THE FLOWERING TREE

THE FLOWERING TREE

Caryll Houselander

CLUNY
Providence, Rhode Island

CLUNY MEDIA EDITION, 2023

This Cluny edition is a republication of the
1945 Sheed & Ward edition of *The Flowering Tree*.

"The Little Boy on the Bus," "The Parish First Communions,"
"The Old Woman," and "A Coffin in Church" were previously published
in *The Messenger of the Sacred Heart of Jesus*; "The Adoration of the
Cross" and "Litany to Our Lady," in *Harlem Friendship House News*.

For more information regarding this title
or any other Cluny Media publication,
please write to info@clunymedia.com, or to
Cluny Media, P.O. Box 1664, Providence, RI 02901

VISIT US ONLINE AT WWW.CLUNYMEDIA.COM

ISBN: 978-1685952006

Nihil Obstat: ARTHUR J. SCANLAN, S.T.D., *censor librorum*

Imprimatur: FRANCIS J. SPELLMAN, D.D., *Archbishop, New York*
NEW YORK, MAY 2, 1949

Cover design by Clarke & Clarke
Cover image: Vincent van Gogh, *Pink Peach Trees*
("*Souvenir de Mauve*"), 1888, oil on canvas
Courtesy of Wikimedia Commons

CONTENTS

"Faithful Cross, O tree all beauteous,
Tree all peerless and divine!
Not a grove on earth can show us
Such a flower and leaf as thine."

to Maisie Ward

The idea that I have is that we are really part, as it were, of a vast rhythm, and that when we become more recollected we become more and more conscious of it. It cuts two ways. We can, I think, cultivate recollection by deliberately saying Rhythms or poetry; and when we do this, those thoughts expressed within us rhythmically are heard by our minds in everything round us, even in the traffic in the street.

This I believe to be the secret of the wonderful power for peace in rhythmic prayer, which comes to its utmost possibilities in the prayer which St. Ignatius proposes, which is finally just rhythmic breathing, and which was practiced by Russian "starets" long before St. Ignatius lived.

The reason why I started to write Rhythms myself was that, being constantly distracted and interrupted by people and circumstances, I made up my mind long ago that it was necessary to discover ways to pray unceasingly *without* the amount of solitude and peace that one desires, and the first thing I thought necessary was to have a peaceful Rhythm always in the mind, some measure that would keep the harmony and balance of music around one's thoughts and emotions, in order that one should not be shattered or disturbed by things round one. But then I found out that since one can't simply *dismiss* one's environment, it must be caught up and woven into the Rhythm. That is why so many of mine are nothing else but descriptions of what is going on around me. "Low Mass on Sunday," for example, could as truly be called "Distractions at Mass."

I discovered, after a time, that other people found themselves soothed and brought into harmony by reading Rhythms, and that certain passages would haunt them; and when they did so, they seemed to have precisely the same power of rocking them into prayer as they had for me. Then I started deliberately to put into Rhythm things and truths which I wanted to be woven right into people's being. That is why so many of mine have shameless repetitions, even word for word sometimes, of passages I have written in prose.

It is, when one thinks of it, very much on the same principle as telling nursery rhymes to children, using them to soothe them to sleep. Rhythm somehow pats to sleep all the trouble and fret of life and rocks us in the arms of God.

I have for a long time felt that a kind of communion of contemplation among us all is what is needed in the world, and I deliberately write Rhythms and give them to all sorts of people in order to start some recollection in their souls.

But apart from being *heard* in the mind, I think a Rhythm, and perhaps more especially a prayer one, has to be one which can be *seen.* Things that look very affected, such as putting one word on a line now and then, are done on purpose. It is to stress things immediately, to show at one *look,* what must just pass through the mind, and what one must pause on. Of course I am not always *right* in my emphasis, and I daresay that I have got into the habit of setting them out like that owing to my inability to punctuate; but at all events people can read them, and they read them as I want them to. It is really on the same lines as writing music with different note values, chords and such, and with counterpoint. I am not at all musical, though I am exceedingly fond of *certain* musicians, but I can take the keenest pleasure in *looking* at musical scores. That is all a bit beside the point, but I have long wanted to point out to you that Rhythm is not, in my mind, simply a freer way of writing verse, but is a part of a plan for contemplation to be spread in the world.

Caryll Houselander

author's note

These Rhythms are not intended to be poems in a new form but simply thoughts, falling naturally into the beat of the Rhythm which is all round us and which becomes both audible and visible in the seasons of the year, the procession of day and night and the liturgical cycle. They are arranged so that the Rhythm and stress will be easily seen as well as thought, by people who are unused to reading verse. The theme which recurs in them is the flowering of Christ in man.

the sermon on the mount

Matthew Speaks

I.

His fame had spread through Syria like flame in dry grass.
From Galilee and the Decapolis and over Jordan the
  people came.
Crowds came out of Judea and out of Jerusalem.

In the hearts of the old men
hope for the race smouldered again:
"Oh, that Messiah were come to set us free!"
In the hearts of the women
hope for the children flickered with faint flame:
"Oh, that Messiah were come to set them free!"
The proud heart of youth blazed, suddenly on fire:
"Oh, for our own glory, in the glory of Messiah!"

I was afraid,
I, the tax-collector,
who had sat in the custom house.
I knew men through and through,
having got my living, as it were,
by other men's despair.

I knew the humiliated;
I knew the oppressed;
I knew the king,
whom they had crowned already
in their desire:
they had created him
out of their bitterness.

Out of their broken flesh,
out of their hunger and thirst,
out of their chains—
weaponless, they had forged him a sword;
ragged, they had woven for him
purple raiment and cloth of gold for a king:
out of the festering wound,
out of the conqueror's scorn,
in dreams,
the son of the race was born—
Messiah, the Son of Dreams.

I knew it all.
How often I had sat in the market-place
and seen the women there, rocking to and fro,
like those who sit by the dead to weep—
rocking, rocking, rocking,
to and fro;
trying to rock the cradled nothingness
in the barren womb
to sleep.

As for the young,
they wanted a leader, whose power
would be in his lust for power,
one whose tongue
would utter their dumb pride
in song
one in whose heart
their frightened hearts would beat
to the sound of drums.

II.

I was afraid
that they would despair
when they saw the Lord.

He was very poor.
He had the chiselled features
of one who denies himself;
His hands
were the large hard hands
of an artisan—
and without a sword;
His eyes,
the eyes of pity and love;
His speech,
the broad, slow speech
of a countryman.

I was afraid.
But when He began to speak
it seemed to each who heard
that the word was spoken to him alone.

He dawned on the people;
He did not take them by storm:
soft as the blown thistledown's sowing,
of the seed of the Word was sown.

Each who heard
knew the light growing within him,
like morning,

slowly welling
and filling the empty sky
before the first song
of the first bird.

I understood,
when He began to teach,
why first
He had given light to blind eyes;
and to deaf ears,
the music of water and wind;
and to hands and feet that were numb,
the touch of the delicate grass and the sun;
and speech to the dumb.

For He spoke of the things
men see and taste and hold:
of salt and rock and light
and the wheat in gold;
of winds and wings and flowers
and the fruit on boughs;
of candle-light in the house.

They heard His voice,
like the voice of a murmurous sea
a long way off, washing the shores of peace:

but each knew within him
a soundless music,
a voiceless singing,
saying:

"Feel the pulse of My love
with your finger-tips;
prove My tenderness
in the tiny beat
of the heart of the mother bird;
lay your hand
on the hard bark of the tree—
know Me
in the rising sap
of the green life in the dark.

"I have strewn the flowers
under your feet:
see if I love you:
see if My love is sweet!"

There was a thawing then,
like the melting of frost
when winter is done
and the warm sun
kisses the world.

There was a thawing then
in the hearts of the women,
and after the hard frost
of the hard years,
their unshed tears
were flowing.

They understood
how the Lord
takes the loveliest least
for His self-bestowing.

They would remember,
when they were baking bread,
how He had said
that His grace
works secretly in them,
like yeast.

When they sifted the ash
and blew the spark of the fire,
they would remember
the Breath of the Spirit
that fans the smoking flax.

He spoke of chastity,
the splendour of love;
of desire,
silver purified
in the heart of the fire;
of thought,
white linen spread
for the marriage feast.

Then
the men knew,
with a great sighing of joy,
that the dead bough
must fall from the living tree:
the fetid thought,
the furtive word,
the seeping lust,
the cloying grief,
the blight on the green leaf,
the hard fruit
with soft rot at the core,
would be no more, no more.

But the heart would be born again
to a white maying and morning
and first falling in love.

III.

Christ looked at the people.
He saw them assailed by fear:
He saw the locked door;
He saw the knife in the hand;
He saw the buried coin;
He saw the unworn coat,
consumed by moth;
He saw the stagnant water
drawn and kept in the pitcher,
the musty bread in the bin—
the defended,
the unshared,
the ungiven.

He told them then
of the love
that casts out fear,
of the love that is four walls
and a roof over the head:
of the knife in the sheath,
of the coin in the open hand,
of the coat given
warm with the giver's life,
of the water poured in the cup,
of the table spread—

the undefended,
the shared,
the given—
the Kingdom of Heaven.

Christ looked at the people.
He saw the hard years
graven upon their faces;
He saw the old clothes,
worn to the shape of their work;
He saw their unshed tears;
He saw the labourer's hands,
hollowed out by the tools
as His own were hollowed out
by the mallet to cup the nail.

He saw the crust of the will,
like the hard crust of rye;
He saw the flesh and blood,
the sacramentels of love;
He saw the image of God,
the crystal in the rock.

He lifted
His large and beautiful hands
to bless.

God abides in men

God abides in men,
There are some men who are simple;
they are fields of corn:
we see the soil and the stubble
more than the green spears
and the yellow stocks.
Such men have minds
like wide grey skies:
they have the grandeur
that the fool calls emptiness.

God is clothed in homespun in such lives.
He goes with them to the field and the barn;
He comes home when the birds,
in dark orderly flocks,
cross the empty twilights of time.

God abides in men.
Some men are not simple:
they live in cities
among the teeming buildings,
wrestling with forces
as strong as the sun and the rain:
often they must forego dream upon dream;
the glare of the electric light
blinds their eyes to the stars.

On some nights
the stir of life and the lights
is a soft fire, like wine
in their blood.

Christ walks again in the wilderness
in such lives,
wrestling with Lucifer,
the fallen angel of Light,
who shows Him the cities of the world,
and with brilliant and illimitable audacity,
offers to Christianity
lordship of the cities,
on the world's terms.

God abides in men.
There are some men
on whom the sins of the world are laid:
they are conscripted,
stripped, measured and weighed;
taken away from home
and sent to the flood,
the fire, the darkness,
the loneliness of death.

In such men
Christ is stripped of His garments;
the reed is put in His hand,
the soldier's cloak on His shoulders,
the cross on His back.
In them He is crucified:
from the lives
and the deaths
of those men
cities rise from the dead.

God abides in men
because Christ has put on
the nature of man like a garment
and worn it to His own shape.

He has put on everyone's life.
He has fitted Himself to the little child's dress,
to the shepherd's coat of sheepskin,
to the workman's coat,
to the king's red robes,
to the snowy loveliness of the wedding-garment,
and to the drab
of the sad, simple battle-dress.

Christ has put on man's nature
and given him back his humanness,
worn to the shape
of limitless love
and warm from the touch
of His life.

He has given man His crown,
the thorn that is jewelled
with drops of His blood.
He has given him
the seamless garment
of His truth.
He has bound him
in the swaddling bands
of His humility.
He has fastened his hands

to the tree of life.
He has latched his feet
in crimson sandals,
that they move not
from the path of love.

God abides in men.

the young man

There is a young man
who lives in a world of progress.
He used to worship a God
Who was kind to him.
The God had a long, white beard.
He lived in the clouds.
But, all the same,
He was close to the solemn child
who had secretly
shut Him up in a picture book.

But now
the man is enlightened.
Now he has been to school
and has learnt to kick a ball
and to be abject
in the face of public opinion.

He knows, too,
that men are hardly removed from monkeys.
You see, he lives in the light
of the twentieth century.

He works twelve hours a day
and is able to rent a room
in a lodging house
that is not a home.

At night he hangs
a wretched coat
upon a peg on the door
and stares
at the awful jug and basin
and goes to bed.
And the poor coat,
worn to the man's shape—
round-shouldered and abject—
watches him, asleep,
dreaming of all
the essential,
holy things
that he cannot hope to obtain
for two pounds ten a week.

Very soon
he will put off his body,
like the poor, dejected coat
that he hates.
And his body will be
worn to the shape
of twelve hours' work a day
for two pounds ten a week.

If he had only known
that the God in the picture book
is not an old man in the clouds,
but the seed of life in his soul;
the man would have lived,
and his life would have flowered
with the flower of limitless joy.

But he does not know,
and in him
the Holy Ghost
is a poor little bird
in a cage,
who never sings
and never opens his wings,
yet never, never
desires to be gone away.

a tree in the city

At last on the little black tree
in the city square
there is a green leaf.

Hesitating,
a ray of the sun comes down.
It is a white finger of light,
pointing to life.

In the offices
the row of pale faces are lifted;
they are turned to the green spark—
unlit candles, wistful for flame.

They are not dreaming
merely of the distant countryside—
of the multitudinous grass,

of passing loveliness.
They know that loveliness
runs out, even through privileged hearts,
like sand through an hour-glass.
They want to begin to *live*,
and to live forever.

The spark of life
in each of their souls
is a gem in a locked casket.

It suddenly burns more brightly,
waxes and wanes,
like a breathing ember.

Now it could be fanned to a great flame
by a mere breath.

Will *no one* come
into the city of London
with the gift in his breath
to answer
the people's wordless supplication
for Life?

mediocracy

All the young men
and all the young women
hope for security,
a mild prosperity,
respectability,
and a dull old-age.

They want the Sunday smell—
beef in a dead street—
six days to be bored
and one to over-eat.

Poor little birds in a cage,
sitting behind the bars!
It isn't life:
it's the living wage
and the night without the stars.

woman with a jug

There is a woman,
an old woman, who shuffles along
with a jug for a pint of beer,
almost oblivious,
seeking oblivion.

Her hair is in metal curlers
under an old tweed cap.
Her face is the poor face
of someone drowned in the sea.

She has never been young,
and her mind is dumb,
and she does not see.
She only floats to the surface,
a terrible accusation to me.

A poor drowned, bloated face,
floating up from the sea
of accepted misery.

And I,
who lower my eyes for shame
as I go by,
am more ashamed
because I wonder why
Despair
troubles to curl her hair.

the little boy on the bus

The little boy on the bus
all alone,
standing with old-world courtesy
to give his seat to a lady,
is fragile, like a leaf.
He seems as if a little breeze
could carry him out of the world:
as if his ribs,
that must be fine filigree
of ivory,
will snap in the heavy crush
of people crowding the bus,
thoughtless and unaware.

Suddenly I turn away.
I could weep,
so beautiful is the old-world courtesy

that blossoms again and again,
like an unassuming rhyme,
changing the human race
from incoherence to song
and to melody;
so strong
is the visible frailty
of the child,
who keeps the sweetness of childhood
in a world of sophistication,
where (it seems to the heartsore)
childhood has no place.

It is in the hands of God:
it seems like a thin glass bowl
of incomparable beauty
in the hands of a connoisseur;
a bowl that was filled with wine
on many a festive board,
that has travelled in ships at sea,
has shone in the distant lands
and forgotten days—
enduring through time,
unbroken.

Exquisite miracle
that had so easily shattered!
still—in its whole perfection—
held in the tender hands
of Infinite Love.

the parish first communions

In the church
there is a smell of flowers.
There are white veils,
and the banners
and the vestments are white.

Why are there tears
in the eyes of the grown-up people?

Have we forgotten
the fragrance of Christ's first coming?
or the stainless hearts
of our little sons and daughters?

Or is it that we remember
that we too were young
and once had a secret with Him?

I am back again
in the French convent
and the austere, lovely morning,
thrilled with the mute mystery
of the day of the First Communions—
the touch of cold water,
the curtains around the beds,
and the clean bare boards
of the floor in the dormitory.

I know that sin is something
to be resisted strongly,
with all my heart.
I have the knowledge of innocence,
learned by watching the flame
in the pale-faced nun
who taught me the lesson of sacrifice.

She smells of lemon and soap and linen.
Her smile is an inward smile,
and her eyes of radiance
teach the innocent heart,
beating with austere joy,
that sin is a terrible thing,
redeemed by a passion of love.

There is a smell of flowers
filling the cloister.
We are moving slowly in ranks.
We are wearing long, white veils
and brides' dresses, down to our feet.
The thin, melodious singing
is the singing of angels
in the green paradise
of children in love.

And afterwards there is breakfast,
the breakfast for feasts,
with roses on the table
and the crimson May outside,
and a bird whose singing
fills my heart.

I think that my heart would break
for joy of that bird singing
right inside it,
were it not that the nun
restrains it with recollection—
and we must have perfect manners
and sit so straight at table.
There is a smell of coffee
and warm new rolls,

and each of us will have a banana
because of the feast.

I am back again
in the French convent
and the austere, lovely morning,
thrilled with the mute mystery
of the day of the First Communions.

low Mass on Sunday

The church is noisy with shuffle of children's feet
and somebody's endless cough.
The heads of the boys in rows
are knobs of unpolished wood—
mahogany, teak, and pine.
Only the little Belgian
son of the delicatessen
has an ebony polished knob.

A tiny girl has come late;
she is wearing a grown-up hat
and a jersey down to her knees.
The benches are full, but still
there is room for the little girl,
as an old, old mumbling man,
who is small like a withered berry,
shrinks smaller still for her sake.

A thin young mother is smiling
while, fidgeting on her lap,
her grave round baby grabs
and puts on his father's hat.
He is staring with shadowless eyes
immense in solemnity.
But the rigid father, dismayed,
gives him a rosary
for plaything, in case he cries:
gives him a string of beads
because they are bright and small
to fit the size of his hand:
as God, the Father of all,
to us, the witless and weak,
gives gently the Mysteries
of the life of His only Son,
to hush the possible cries
of spirits too small to hold
the simplicity of His love.

We are the common bread;
we are flesh and blood;
we are salt.
It is strange to think that the saints,
with their delicate smile of peace
carved in stone, and the flowers

withering at their feet,
were also the common bread
and were flesh and blood
and were salt.

Not with the crystal peace
held up to receive the light
we come, but tangled with care.
Deep in the earth our roots,
locked in the earth we know.

We are knit by a single thread,
a rhythm of fear—we are one
at least in this, like the many
separate leaves on a bough,
turned by a gust of wind
to a single fluttering wave:
the fear between night and day,
before the singing of birds,
before the flood of the rose
sweeps the monotonous grey
that is filling the window-pane;
before the will is awake
and the face for the world put on
with the hated ill-fitting clothes,
grotesque with the body's shape;

the fear when the mouths of the children
burn to malignant flowers,
crimson-black in a fever;
the wordless dread when the old,
who are kind, like leaves in the autumn
fade from their lovely russet
and are thin and crumpled and brown,
frail as leaves on the wind-drift,
suddenly dropping down;
fear when the work is uncertain,
in peril the precious home
and the wretched rags of respect
for the shivering thing called self;
the piteous fear in the heart,
guarding a secret guilt
from one whose faith, if it failed,
would kill at last, with its failing,
the shoot that struggles up
from the soil of the crippled mind
to flower in the day, unashamed.

Monotony of the things
that link the years of a life
like an ever-recurring rhyme,
dragging a commonplace poem
through a wearisome repetition

that dulls the mind to its sense:
it seems like a worn-out story
that beggars tell in the street and nobody
   still believes.

The priest goes up to the altar:
he is not a priest of gold or of ivory;
he does not wear a chasuble stiff with pearls
or a halo of golden red;
he does not move in a cloud's mysterious blue;
he is not the priest of the picture books
of the heretics,
of the pagans.
He is a little man of our flesh and blood:
he knows what it is to have to scrape and to save;
he talks to mothers about the cost of living;
he is bald, and his polished crown
reflects the sanctuary lamp
in marbles of light that move
on its pinkness round and round.
He can be impatient—and kind;
he can comfort—and scold;
he is flesh and blood;
he is salt.
But his short hands, red with cold
and chapped by the same hard water

that we all use at home,
are the hands that must lift up God.

He is bowed and beating his breast,
and Christ is among us:
His hands of a workman, extended—
the bone and the sinew,
the line and the beauty,
of labourers' hands—
opening slowly,
revealing a wound:

His coming as gentle
as naked feet walking
on snow newly fallen.
Now
we can guess at the secret of God.
He has vested Himself for His Mass
in the rags of our nature,
and we are vested in Him.

Our fears are not, after all,
something to push out of sight,
madmen behind the bars:
in the lifted hands of Christ
our wounds are solitary stars,

answering, out of the night,
to the Light of God.

And we
are here on the cross.
The nails are so gentle,
the wood is so tender,
the scourge falls so lightly,
when Christ
lifts to the Father
the hands that have nothing
to offer themselves.
His fingers close fondly,
embracing the nails.

How seldom we ponder
the words that were spoken
to teach us and comfort.
"Consider the flowers of the field,
and the birds of the air."

Yet there
on the ash heap, behind the back garden,
sown by the wind is a flower
lifting its supplication
out of the dust and rubbish.

The wind sows the seed,
and how seldom
we think of the flower of the spirit!
The birds sing in London;
a blackbird with three notes like water,
in three shining marbles of crystal,
sang only today in our garden.
The pigeons pace, solemn and gentle,
sparrows still hop in the gutter;
flight, winging over the chimneys,
sweeps the same wonder of rhythm
as flight on the unclouded blueness
ringing Love's head, when His blessing,
like slow drops of rain in the summer,
fell on the lowly forever,
on each aspiration and sorrow
known to the minds that adore Him.

The saints, like white constellations,
burn in their passion of glory,
but we in our prayers are homely,
like the wax candles
that burn on the altar.
As full are the flames of the candles
as stars, in their fulness of light,
full in their flame and their golden

and mute adoration.
It comes from the earth;
it speaks dumbly
of wax that is simple,
of honey
and droning of bees
in walled gardens.
First-fruits we bring to the altar
of God, who gives joy to our youth,
and years that are mellow and turning
like flowers, that turn in the waning
of day to the last ray of light,
and fold their thin petals till morning.
The goodness of earth and the beauty
of things that are simple and holy.
Christ is among us,
His heart like a rose
expanding within us,
alone in the sunlight.

The voice of the priest, growing urgent,
says to us, "Lift up your hearts,"
and we say, "They are lifted."
The wandering thoughts of the server
are gathering into a circle
crowning his heart, like the bees

round a red flower, where the honey
with sweetness invites them.
With his hands of a child he lifts gently
the edge of the chasuble, waiting,
waiting for Love's crucifixion.
In the poor hands with their roughness,
the fingers misshapen with chilblains,
Christ, the white bread of the simple,
is lifted, and we are all lifted.

Like bowstrings, taut for the arrow,
the ribs of Christ drawn fine.

The arrow is sped:
He has winged it
out of our sorrow,
out of our dying daily,
out of our night:
it has wounded
the Heart Uncreated,
Love with Love
and Light with Light.

Like sunlight in June in an orchard,
a smile of mute peace thrills through us,
the multitude of the leaves

are separate flames of the beauty
of Undivided Light.

That done, once more the shuffling
begins again, and the coughing,
everyone shifting a little,
relieved that the moment of glory—
though never ending—
is ended.
The organ is groaning and wheezing,
the schoolmistress panting and singing
"Sweet Heart of Jesus" with fury,
to stimulate juvenile bleating.

And Christ, with desire,
waits eagerly;
Christ, with patience, awaits
our Communion and His:
like a gathered blade of wheat
in the hand of a child,
the prisoner who is free,
the wings
that are folded,
waiting our coming—
illimitable love,
waiting the clumsy,

hesitating,
limited,
blind
embrace.

They are not more blessed
whose feet
are set on the mountain path,
who abide in the cloud,
content with the touch
of a God who is featureless,
than we who, weaker in faith,
learn by touching His wounds
in the human race
that our hands
touch with His power to heal:
than we, at the wedding
of earth and Heaven,
turning the water to wine
by a fling of the heart
to God—
in the lowliest,
in the nearest at hand.

We are the simple bread
ground for the simpler Host.

What is a little fear,
returning again and again,
and need
and a measure of joy,
but the thirst
and the rain
in the summer heat,
maturing the wheat
for the Host?
We are the common salt
wherewith must the earth be salted.

Now we may go,
and He,
with the hands of a workman,
the hands of a child,
will beat on the heart's low door
wherever we are.
And we
the words of Incarnate Love,
whispered and tuned to ears
deaf to the song of angels,
will answer with tidings of joy.

The rows of the little boys
and the pale-faced, twittering girls

follow their gaudy banner
to the sudden glare of the street,
and follow the good old men
who served at the Mass when they
had wooden bullets for heads,
and the women who tell the priest
stories of operations
and visions he doesn't believe.

In the church,
welling like water
rising in a grey stone well,
silence gathers.

"Will You come down from the cross,
Jesus of Nazareth?
If You are God, will You come down,
down from the cross,
where we are all lifted,
drawing all men to Your heart?"
He remains alone
in the silence.

God remains on the cross,
among the invisible wings
of the legions of angels

thronging the solitude.
He holds them back with His hands,
the hands of a workman,
the hands of a child:
His fingers close on the nails.
God remains on the cross,
alone in the solitude—
illimitable Love,
smiling and smiling.

schoolgirls

On the teacher's desk
a few flowers
are fading in a jam pot.
They were brought by the little new girl,
who worships the teacher.
She held them too long and too tight
in her hot and clammy hand—
the little girl with lifeless hair
who is not listening to the lesson
but is abandoned to the drug
of the teacher's melodious voice.

The voice is swamping her being:
it is covering water,
bearing her away;
she is drowning blissfully

because she floats too easily
with the tide.

She resembles the withering flowers—
an only child
brought up too long at home
by a widowed mother:
now her mother is dead.
The child has the pallor
of a flowering weed
grown in a dark cellar.

Because her mother
refused to admit that she squinted,
she now wears horn-rimmed glasses.
Because she is weak
and defenseless
she is hated.

Her eyes are vacant,
the pupils only pinpoints,
the pale blue circles, paler,
filled with light.
She is dreaming.

She is on the railway track,
gathering buttercups
to give to the teacher.
There is the teacher!
crossing the line
on the level crossing.
A train is coming!
Yes! it is the express!
The buttercups are scattered—
gold largesse of love:
the little girl rushes out
and saves the teacher.

Now the child is dead—
not crushed
but whole
and beautiful.
She is a Roman martyr
decorated with the George Medal.
The teacher, kneeling beside her,
weeps.
Her comrades,
abashed in their admiration
and mute remorse,
stand round the bier

in a circle,
hanging their heads.

The teacher has spoken twice!
Now she is angry.
The little new girl is blushing,
not having heard the question.
Everyone titters;
someone is passing a note;
everyone turns and stares.
She does not care,
that teacher,
if the child would die for her
on the railway line:
she only cares about the noun
that she can't decline.

The flowers fade in the jam pot;
their heads hang down;
the heart of the little girl
is withering,
withering in the driving wind
of the teacher's indifference
and the ridicule of her comrades.

The class is over;
they are all about her;
her secret is torn from her—
her inviolate love
fingered by mocking fingers.
They have torn off her garments,
the threadbare of her reserve:
she is naked now.
They have cast lots on her garments;
they have surrounded her;
they peck at her heart
like a flock
of dark and evil birds
pecking a scarlet cherry
which, by a miracle,
ripened on a blighted tree.

Suddenly they are silent:
the teacher is coming.
Even now she may smile
or speak
or rebuke
the child
(even rebuke would be sweet).

The teacher passes by.
She accepts as her due,
as a queen accepting a vassal's homage,
the innocent
and defenseless passion
of first love.
Unaware,
in her inordinate vanity,
she walks on the heart
that bleeds in the dust,
a scattered rose
whose petals are drops of blood.

The girls adore her.
She walks
on the rush and sweetness
of wild invisible springs,
with steps that crush,
not one season of life,
but season on tender season.
And the net-ball captain,
who is too healthy
and wholly without reticence,
is privileged
to carry her books to the door.

She has gone.
The monotony
of the meaningless hours—
the endless,
timeless time—
descends.

In the empty classroom
the flowers in the jam pot
are dying.
The little new girl weeps.
Already she is a thin and awkward woman,
rejecting love
because she is afraid
of being rejected.

The children
creep round the window—
tittering,
sniggering,
pointing,
like dark and evil birds
who have again seen
the scarlet cherry
grown by a miracle
on a tree that is blighted.

A score of glittering eyes
pierce the solitude of her grief;
yet she remains alone
in an empty
and timeless world,
weeping and weeping.

walterton road

Twilight is full of laughter
here in Walterton Road,
where the children swarm on the steps
and the washing hangs in rows.

How sharp the life is
that burns in the thin women
calling from door to door;
it has defeated the world—
but with a sting,
not with sweetness;
they are like wild nettles,
growing green in the ashes.

Yet how sweet the life is
here, in the boy and girl
in their time of maying.

But shrineless the bread
for the Sacrament—
shame on the jaundiced eyes
denying homeless love
its oblivious kiss in the street!

Brave is the young mother;
very brave in her life is.
She sits in the window
and twists, with a laughing finger,
the baby's feather of hair;
he pulls the geranium flower,
and drops the petals down
on the boy and girl
in a crimson shower.

Does anyone ever guess
when the watch ticking over his
heart marks his loveliest hour?

Twilight is full of laughter,
and there in a dark frame
of a tenement windowpane
a yellow canary sings
in a yellow cage.

The rooms are crowded here,
and the walls weep:
there is no solitude.
Birth meets death
and pushes past on the stairs.
It is always washing and cooking
and trying to make ends meet
and carping cares;
but life springs up like a weed;
life is a green shoot,
springing up everywhere.

What hands are here!
what hard, labouring hands,
warding off blows
and defending—
what eyes for a vision!
What hearts for a Resurrection!
What lives there are—
sharp, like spears, forefending
foes that threaten a spark
which will still be burning
after the last star.

Look!
the blue purity

over the chimney pots:
listen!
the children's laughter,
scattering shadows.

Oh, brooding Spirit of God,
Breath of the Wind
that blows wherever it will,
ruffling the rags of life a little
and then
zephyr,
here in a sheltered valley
and still.

the old woman

The old woman who nods by the altar
is plain and ill-shapen,
and her clothes musty.
She thinks her life useless.
She has scrubbed many floors,
and always she did it mostly
for God's glory,
but never with the vision
that makes the work easy.

She is changed to dull copper
by the light of the candles
lit at the feet of the saints
by the children.
She is twisted and ugly
like an old apple tree
that long has forgotten

the sweetness of blossom
and fruit in the sunlight—
old black bark
of a tree that is leafless.

She knows that the priest,
with eyes averted,
thinks her a nuisance—
garrulous, tedious,
talking of rheumatics.

The middle-aged mystics pass her with pity.
She fumbles her rosary and mumbles Hail Marys
with tongue that is garrulous
and mind that is drowsy.

"What shall I do,"
she thinks very dully,
"when my rheumatics keep me indoors
never any more, in the kind courts of Heaven,
to sit in a corner, content to be nothing?"

And Christ, in the silence,
in the silence of twilight,
with still voice of silver,
unheeded, answers:

"I will find My beloved—
the whiteness of blossom,
the young boughs laden,
sap in the branches,
the azure above her.
I will find My beloved
when all the leaves singing
are voices of birds
in My Father's keeping—
the sap in the branches,
the young boughs laden,
and My hand beneath her
and My heart above her."

a coffin in church

By the sanctuary
there is a small coffin.
It is draped with a violet pall,
and round it
four candles burn,
four flames of peace.

I cannot guess
the hidden features,
but I think that they are smiling,
because they have passed
through the valley
of the shadow of death.

And the Blessed,
with extended hands,
welcome

the soul that is crystal,
reflecting
Light
from the purifying fire,

The haloes of the Blessed
are the lights
across the water
from the shore
that shelters
the last harbour,
like the crook
of a lover's curved arm,
holding the Beloved
at rest.

And the angels,
with their wings crowding,
come like flocking birds
to guide a sparrow
from its rifled nest
to the sun.

And Mary, God's Mother,
with mild almond-eyes
that laugh softly,

sees but a child
in a cradle,
waiting
for the morning
to wake it.

I, who am still
in the valley
of the shadow
of death,
fondly speed him:
"Go forth swiftly,
Christian soul!
to meet the crowned Lord,
Who is crowned with the thorn
in flower.

"Go forth,
like Lazarus,
who was once poor!"

joseph

Since Joseph has worn
his coat of many colours
he is hated by his brothers;
yet love is in his heart,
like a fountain rising.

He is hated by the philistine
because he is a singer:
the sound of machines
is the proper music
of progress and commerce,
but he sings of the crystal
shining in the rock
in silence and darkness,
and his song echoes
through the heart of the world—
like a bird-song

scattering
wild-wasted loveliness
through an empty room
where a dead man is lying.

He is hated by the pharisee
because he is a mourner
and by the sealed tombs
of the souls of the sinners
he sees the thorn lying,
the nails and the sceptre,
of a king laid in state:
and he brings spikenard
in jars of jade,
like the sea-waters,
and pours out lavishly
the salt of his tears.

He is hated by the cynic
because he is a poet,
beholding the mystery
of the mountain flowers
and the intricate loveliness
of the white snowflake,
melting in the sunrise
of the new morning.

He is hated by those
who live in security,
wanting for nothing
but the one thing needed;
because, with his hands
that seem to be empty,
he scatters the seed
that springs in the gutter
and that only the children
and the innocent
may gather.

He is hated by the fearful
because he is fearless
and the rush of his wings
on their way to the sun
bears up a heart beating in ecstasy
on the barred gate of Life
that the world calls death.

Since Joseph has worn
his coat of many colours
he is hated by his brothers—
yet love is in his heart
like a fountain rising.

litany to our Lady

Lady, giver of Bread,
Christ-bestowing,
give us the Bread of Life!

Fallow land for the sowing,
darkness over the seed,
secrecy for the growing:
give us the Living Bread.

Empty cup for the wine,
white linen, spread
without fold for the feast:
give us the Bread of Heaven,
yeast and leaven,
Christ-bestowing:
give us to eat.

Give us the Bread in the wheat,
Lady, giver of Bread.

Full grape in the vine,
give us the strong Wine
poured into the chalice
and lifted up.

Drained cup,
give us the broken Bread;
give us the crust of sorrow,
hard as rye,
Christ-bestowing.

Give us the emptiness
of the dark furrow,
while the great wind
of the Spirit is blowing
and sowing seed.

Lady, giver of Bread,
field sown by the wind,
snow white on the field,
darkness under the snow:
yield
the Bread of Life!

Wheat, leaven and yeast
and wine for the feast:
give us the Bread of Life,
Lady, giver of Bread,
Christ-bestowing.

philip speaks

*Dedicated, in gratitude, to Dr. J. W. Mackail, O. M., in whose hands
all that is good in "Philip Speaks" has been multiplied*

When we returned and told Him all we had done,
I, for one, was emptied out like a husk
that has scattered its seed upon hard ground.

We had not had time even to eat;
always the open hand,
always the blind eyes,
always the deaf ears,
always the wound to be healed.

My thoughts were like wild birds
beating the bars of the cage
for empty skies.

Even now the smell of the people
clung to my hair and clothes.

A rotten sweetness of oil and musk
that smells like death, it hung in my hair.

Their voices went on and on in my head,
monotonous waves wearing my mind away.
(Rock is worn by the waves to sand.)
I wanted to shut my mind, that my thoughts might close
on my own peace; I wanted to close
the peace of my love in my heart,
like dew in a dark rose.

He told us to rest.

We went in a small ship,
the wind and water moving in her.
She lived in their sweetness of life, a bride.
Her sail, a white wing—unmoving—moved with the tide.
She lay to the wind, and we gave our hearts with a sigh
to the breath of the Spirit of Love.

But when we came to the shore
the people were there;
they had found us out:
always the open hand,
always the blind eyes,
always the deaf ears,

always the wounds to be healed!
They were there,
swarming there, everywhere—
insects there in the sun
when someone has lifted a stone.
I knew they would drain Him
and wring Him out—wring Him out
to the last drop of the fountain-water of Life.
I was sick of it all,
with a dry husk for a heart.

But He saw the flocks wanting shepherd and fold;
pity in Him rose in a clear spring
for the world's thirst, and love was a pastureland.

So it went on all day:
always the open hand,
always the dull mind,
always the slow heart,
always the nameless fears;
and self-pity, self-pity and tears;

until the sun went up in the blaze of the day's heat,
and with red wine burning through thin gold,
it was lowered slowly onto the altar-stone
of the darkening world, where the sheep were in fold.

We thought, "Now it is night; He will send them away;
the hour is late." We said, "This is a desert place.
Send them away, Lord, to buy food and be fed!"
But He: "You give them to eat!"

The grass in that place shone exceedingly green.
I remember, because when the brain is dust
the cool greenness of grass is absurdly sweet.
"There is a lad here," said Andrew,
"with two little fish and five loaves of bread.
But what are these, if this crowd must be fed?"
"Bid them sit down on the grass, and give them to eat,"
    the Lord said.

The lad was one of the crowd; he went as he came.
As long as the world lasts, the world will remember him,
but no one will know his name!

They sat down on the grass.
My heart contracted; my mind was withered up;
but Christ poured out His tenderness,
like wine poured out into a lifted cup.

Always the open hands,
always the blind eyes,
always the mouth to be fed;

and I, for one, was emptied out like a husk
that has scattered its seed upon hard ground.
But He saw the flocks wanting shepherd and fold;
pity in Him rose in a clear spring
for the world's thirst, and love was a pastureland.

The Lord blessed the bread.
He put it into our hands
and it multiplied,
not in *His* hands but in *mine*!
Even now, remembering this,
my thoughts shut like a folding wing;
my mind is a blank sheet of light
in the mystery of the thing.

I gave, and my hands were full, again and again;
pity in Him fell on my dry dust:
it was summer rain,
and the husk of my heart expanded and filled again
and was large with grain.

For me, the miracle was this:
that a clear stream of the Lord's love—
not mine—
flowed out of my soul,
a shining wave over my fellow men.

These things I have told you happened a long while since.
Our cherished Lord is dead; He was crucified.
Now, as then, we go about in the crowd, telling His love
and how He rose from the dead and, risen in us,
He lives in the least of men.
But I think nobody understands,
until I touch their wounds and they know
the healing of *His* hands.

On the night of the Pasch, before He died,
He blessed the bread and put it into my hands,
to increase and be multiplied to the end of time.

Now, if I turned my face away from the market-place,
I should be haunted,
hearing the rustle of wheat in the darkness—
striving, pushing up to the light.
I should hear His words, falling like slow tears
in the supper-room,
when He prayed that we all be one,
even as they are one, the Father and Son:

falling like slow tears
over the sown fields;
and I should see the world
like a young field of wheat

growing up for the grain,
watered by Christ's tears.

Always the open hands,
always the blind eyes,
always the slow mind,
always the deaf ears,
and always Christ, Our Lord,
crowned with the flowering thorn
and ringed with spears.

I know—now that I never see
the print of His feet in the dust
where the Son of Man trod—
that in every man, forever,
I meet the Son of God.

the reed

She is a reed,
straight and simple,
growing by a lake
in Nazareth:

a reed that is empty,
until the Breath of God
fills it with infinite music:

and the breath of the Spirit of Love
utters the Word of God
through an empty reed.

The Word of God
is infinite music
in a little reed:

it is the sound of a Virgin's heart,
beating in the solitude of adoration;
it is a girl's voice
speaking to an angel,
answering for the whole world;

it is the sound of the heart of Christ,
beating within the Virgin's heart;
it is the pulse of God,
timed by the breath of a Child.

The circle of a girl's arms
has changed the world—
the round and sorrowful world—
to a cradle for God.

She has laid love in His cradle:
in every cot
Mary has laid her Child.

In each
comes Christ;
in each Christ comes
to birth;
comes Christ from the Mother's breast,
as the bird from the sun

returning—
returning again to the tree he knows,
and the nest,
to last year's rifled nest.

Into our hands
Mary has given her Child:
heir to the world's tears,
heir to the world's toil,
heir to the world's scars,
heir to the chill dawn over the ruin of wars.
She has laid Love in His cradle,
answering, for us all,
"Be it done unto me":

The child in the wooden bed,
the light in the dark house,
the life in the failing soul,
the Host in the priest's hands,
the seed in the hard earth,
the man who is child again—
quiet in the burial bands,
waiting his birth.

Mary, Mother of God,
we are the poor soil

and the dry dust;
we are hard with a cold frost.

Be warmth to the world;
be the thaw,
warm on the cold frost;
be the thaw that melts,
that the tender shoot of Christ,
piercing the hard heart,
flower to a spring in us.

Be hands that are rocking the world
to a kind rhythm of love;
that the incoherence of war
and the chaos of our unrest
be soothed to a lullaby;
and the round and sorrowful world,
in your hands,
the cradle of God.

bruges

Bruges!
Oh, my Beloved!
Nest of the Pelican!

Here are still waters,
and bells,
weaving my thoughts
with the solemn joy
of the carillon.
Here are birds
in dark, orderly flocks,
crossing the steeple.
Here is the Host,
nourishing Bread
of a devout people.

All mothering Christ,
Patient Love!
Water and birds and bells
and flowering steeple,
shrine of the gentle God
intimate here with man.

Oh, Bruges!
Oh, my Beloved!
Nest of the Pelican!

When I am far from here,
Bruges,
little city of bells,
keep my heart
in the shrine
with the Sacrament.

When I have gone,
keep my heart
in the peace of the still water,
and my desire heavenward,
growing up from the altar,
with your flowering spires.

When I am far from here,
Bruges,
little city of love,
keep my heart
in the measured beauty
of bells,
ringing their carillon
in the grey steeple.

Keep my heart in the shrine
with the Sacrament,
in communion
with your gentle,
devout people.

the rosary

I.

In the doorway of a low grey house,
built of stones as old as the Crusades,
a woman of Bruges sits in the sunlight,
among the flowers, saying her Rosary.

She seems to be carved out of seasoned walnut
and polished smooth
by the constant touch of the hand of God,
and the beads that twine her crippled fingers
are scarlet berries on the thorny twigs.

The running rhythm
and the repetition
of the *Paters* and the *Aves*
is like the rhythm that in nature
moves through the seasons

from seed to harvest
with the unity
and the pause and stress
of music;
like the bloodstream of Christ,
that flows through the seasons
from Advent to Easter
in the liturgy of the Church,
the ebb and flow of the tide of Love
in the Mystical Body of Christ.

II.

God has given His children strings of beads,
as we give strings of beads to our children,
to teach them to count.

We do not say,
"Learn from these the doctrine of numbers,
the measure of human life,
the dream of Pythagoras,
counting the pulse of the world."

We do not say
to a child with a string of beads,
"Learn the perfection of reason in mathematics."

We say,
"Learn to count on the beads,
small for your hands to hold,
bright for your eyes to see."
And he begins,
slowly,
with one, two, three:
the spark is kindled
to light the flame of philosophy.

God has counted in fifteen Mysteries,
on the fingers of human creatures,
the singleness of the Undivided Love,
the simplicity
that we cannot comprehend
because our hearts are divided.

III.

We are not all vessels of gold,
lifted up in virginal hands,
empty chalices to receive,
from the perfect vine,
love,
absolute
and complete.

But the old woman of Bruges
is a round bowl,
lifted up to be brimmed
with the pure wine.
And the Mysteries of the Rosary
concern familiar things
known in her own life.
Her mind, like a velvet bee
droning over a rose,
gathers the honey of comfort
from the story of God,
familiar as the things in her kitchen—
the shining pots and pans,
the milk in the jar of earthenware,
and the flags of the scrubbed floor.

The story told by the Rosary
is the story of primitive beauty,
true as the burden of folk-songs.

It is a song piped on the hills,
by a shepherd calling his sheep.

IV.
The cradle of wood,

the wood of the cross;
from cradle to cross,
like a lullaby;
the wail of an infant,
lost on the wind—
the arms of a girl,
in a circle of love,
rocking to rest;
a woman's arms
in a circle of love,
the young Man dead
on His Mother's breast.

The jewels that glow
low in the grass
on the feet of Christ,
risen from death,
touching the flowers
and touching the dust,
even in glory.

The dust of the earth
on the feet of God,
walking the soft blue meadows of stars.

V.

In the doorway of a low grey house,
built of stones as old as the Crusades,
a woman of Bruges
sits in the sunlight, among the flowers,
saying her Rosary.

The story of Mary is her own story,
and her son was her life's joy
and her life's sorrow;
and forever
her son is her life's glory.

In a field in Flanders,
among the red poppies,
he is sleeping:
he will sleep soundly
until the day of resurrection.

She has still the patchwork quilt made,
when her hands were nimble,
for the wooden cot:
now he is sleeping, and each year
he has a new coverlet
of delicate young grass,

and at the end of his cot
a wooden cross.
The cradle of wood,
the wood of the cross;
from cradle to cross,
like a lullaby.

The story of the woman of Bruges
is the world's story.
It is the story
of human joy and sorrow,
woven and interlaced,
like the blue and crimson thread
in a woven cloth:
the story of birth and death,
of war and the rumours of war
and of peace past understanding,
peace in the souls that live
in the life of Christ.

In the doorway in Bruges,
sitting among the flowers,
her mind like a velvet bee
droning over a rose,
taking the honey of comfort
out of the heart of Love,

the old woman is nodding
over her Rosary.

She has lived her meditation,
like the Mother of God,
living the life of Christ:
let her sleep in Christ's peace.

VI.

Under the loud din
of the tramp of metallic feet
in the armed march of time,
like a river moving
under the dark hills,
the everlasting life
is flowing, eternally.

The measured beat of Love,
with pure perfection of music,
timing the life of Christ
in the human heart
goes on.

afternoon in westminster cathedral

I.

In the cathedral
the bones of the martyr
Blessed John Southworth
are laid down low
for our hope and our comfort.

The Church,
in infinite wisdom,
draws the curtains
over the windows of Heaven:
she does not show,
to the newly opened eyes of infancy,
the blazing light of the saints
in glory.

She puts off the jewels
from her ardent bosom,
lest they bruise
the faces of her children;
and she invites
the hard pressure
of the round head
to the tenderness of her heart.

Her jewels are set in the crown
ringing her bowed face,
but in the cradle of her large lap
she treasures a man's bones.

Her gesture of austere tenderness
tells us: "This was a whole man!—
not only a figure painted on a wall,
in a red chasuble, with a halo of gold-leaf."

A whole man is not only a flame
of spiritual fire,
but the holocaust of flesh and blood,
laid on the flame.

The Church treasures a man's bones.

He wanted the plates gleaming,
and the good bread
and the soft wine,
when the stars were a bloom of fire
on the blue dusk;
he wanted the white touch of linen,
caressing his sleep.

He was hungry,
and not only
for the Divine Bread;
he was thirsty,
and not only for the Wine in the chalice;
he was homesick,
and not only
for the Kingdom of Heaven.

Even the shadowless beauty
of the open flower in the light,
gazing upon the sun,
thrusts the roots of its life
downwards into the earth.

He was hunted like the fox;
he was hunted like One
more homeless than the fox—

the little red fox
who is hunted to the death.

He was afraid:
and his heart beat in unison
with the frightened heart of Christ,
facing His death.

In the cathedral,
the bones of the martyr
Blessed John Southworth
are laid down low
for our hope and our comfort.

A whole man
is not only
a flame of spiritual fire
but the holocaust
of flesh and blood,
consumed in the flame.

11.
It is not by chance
that our daily bread
is earned by abnegation

and daily dying,
or that when we have eaten
we hunger for other bread.
We have received the Light of our Life
from the hands of martyrs:
it is not by chance that the Church shows us
a man's bones.

We could not receive
the flame of the Fire of Life
in the hands of dust
were not the hands of dust
scored with the wounds of Christ.

It is not by chance
that the lovers of God
are the poor and the disregarded,
and the world's lovers
possess the world.

The kingdom of God
is not the abundance of things.

That which the moth consumes,
that which the rust rots,
that which the thieves steal,

will be no more:
that which remains is dust,
and a seed in the dust
and a flame.

By the light that we hold in our hand
we look on the face of Love
in a dark glass:
it is the bruised face
having no comeliness
whereby He is known;
it is the bruised face
on the veil of Veronica;
it is the only likeness
left in the world
for the vision of men.

It is not only
the mystery of perfection
that drives us to Him
Who abides in men.

In the struggle for food
we wrestle to come to Him;
we pursue Him blindly,
pursuing our fugitive loves:

it is more than friend and lover
and father and mother
we seek,
when we seek the peace
of communion with one another.

III.

Through the cathedral,
like leaves on a soft wet mist
in the autumn,
the people drift
and are gone again,
to lose their identity
in the uniform greyness
along Victoria Street.
They are extinguished lamps;
they do not burn
with the fire
of their secret glory;
they do not weep;
they are unaware
of their need for the solace of tears.

They come
out of the meaningless fog

of their unexamined lives,
like skeleton-leaves in a mist.
Each supposes himself alone,
but on each
the eyes of a Lover
gaze with intensity,
gaze with the eyes of a mother
watching an only child;
and a heart in the solitude
of the splendour of peace
beats with the selfless passion
of unrequited love.

They are gone,
intent upon nothing.
It is the luncheon hour,
and the eating shops
are thick with steam
and the smell of hair-oil
in dirty hats;
they swarm in the eating shops;
they are earning their daily bread
with the abnegation of the unburied dead.
They eat, but they do not hear
the rustle of Living Wheat
in the breaking of bread.

It is two o'clock.
The people sag,
bored, in the airless office,
watching the clock
that measures the awful boredom;
they do not think
how every tick of the clock
measures the beat of a heart
that knocks on the door of death.

It is six o'clock.
The office disintegrates;
the people hurry away;
the varnished chair,
pushed awry in the hurry to go,
is·empty;
the mouse comes out and dances—
who would care
if so and so never came back again?
Another would come and another,
and always another.

But the Presence follows each one—
an invisible tide
that surges against his heart:
it is like the heat of the sun

beating down through the heavy earth
to the roots of a tree.

If a man would drive his roots
down deep
into the world's incarnate beauty
of flesh and blood,
the thrust would drive him up
to the sun:
from the mould of man's sorrow
the sap would rise in him;
and the tree of his life,
thick with green leaves
and the singing of numberless birds,
would live in the majesty
of the word made flesh.

IV.

Christ is weeping over Jerusalem.
His tears hang in the mist
over the city of London;
His tears water the parched dust
in Spain and in Mexico;
on the white snow of Holy Russia
His tears are frozen,

and the drops of His blood
fall down softly through the snow-drift,
like the leaves of a dark rose.

The world will not serve
a God Who is also a poor man,
Who has chosen
bread and dust
for the revelation of Love.

The world will bow
to a God
Who is out of the reach
of the common people—
remote, like a jewelled ikon
set in a circle of flames,
an ineffectual loveliness
that neither demands nor rebukes.

On the loom of iniquity,
with black and cunning fingers,
the hands of the world have woven
a golden garment
to put on God.

Now, with a gesture
of terrible patience,
Christ submits
to the ignorance
and the misery
of an exasperated people
who think it is He
Who despoiled them:
that the Shepherd struck His sheep
for a tawdry garment of gold,
tarnished with tears.

They dress Him up
like a clown,
in a red cloak.
Over the altar
there is a painted crucifix:
long ago
there was a painted cross
in Russia
and Mexico.

In Spain
there was a crucifix
carved in ivory,
each drop of blood

a dark and tragic garnet,
the hair engraved
and inlaid,
beautiful,
with threads of pure gold.

It is trampled into the mud,
In England
there was a crucifix
carved in wood:
the face was a child's face
that smiled:
the smile was the glow
of the heart that shone with Love.

It is in a museum behind a glass case.

Lifted up,
dire in His poverty,
stark in His nakedness,
nailed like vermin,
Christ is ruling
the inward kingdom.

The kingdom of God
is not

the works of the mind of man
or the gathered treasures of art
or the churches built with hands
or the defended city.

The kingdom of God
is the integrity
of a man's heart.

Lifted up above the ruins
of centuries of the dreams of men,
Christ is ruling upon the cross.

V.

In the cathedral
there is a stab on the grey,
a wound of purple and scarlet,
and the sound of the voices of men.

It is the hour of the Offices of the Church:
the music of David's harp,
the majesty of the Psalms,
that have worn the rocks
of the intellect of the world
to smooth channels

to bear the rivers of Light
to unsounded seas.

It is not only the cadence
of the voices of the priests;
it is not only the murmur
of monks, far away, in their stalls—
monks in black habits and brown and white,
blackbirds and sparrows and doves
in the boughs of the Tree of Life,
hymning the last long hour
of the light;
the separate notes
of the whole of created nature
are brought into harmony:
the sap in the tree,
the leaf, the flower, the seed;
the shaken weed,
stirring a distant star;
the creatures wild in the wood
and the creatures under the sea:
the unconscious world,
proclaiming the Being of Love,
is lit by the spark
of the conscious will of man,
who, with a torch in his hand,

fans its flame
with his breath in the sanctuary.

And we,
syllables of the Word,
are uttering Him
Who utters the secret of God.

It is He
Who lifts
the hands of supplication,
burning with crimson stars;
He Who comes with unsandalled feet
and enters the cloud of fire;
He Who sets the pulse of the world
to the heartbeat of adoration:
He, the Incarnate Word
of Eternal Love
spoken to men,
answers for men
to God.

In Him
we, who are sinners, redeem;
we, who are weak, endure;
we, who tremble, are strong;

we, who falter, accept;
we, who are blind, see;
we, who are deaf, hear;
we, who are dumb, speak;
who, who are nothing, adore.

VI.

There is a young man in the cathedral,
there for want of anywhere else to go.
He is limp, and his trousers sag;
he is a poor little marionette
who would like to dance again
before he is put away in a box
for the night;

he thinks that the Showman
has forgotten His puppet
and nobody pulls the strings;

he thinks that the world is sifting,
like quicksand, under his feet:
he does not know that his feet are upon the rock,
and the rock is worn to a hollow, to cup his tears,
and the rock is split

to receive the wind-sown flower
of his measureless joy.

There is a woman who prays,
as grey as the stone,
without a name or a face;
she assumes a unique majesty,
only by being still
in a world that is ever moving,
moving and ever moving,
on the surge of its own unrest.

She is the still water
in the hollow of the rock
beside the driven sea;
she is the still water
receiving the light.
She is alone,
but in her strong hands
she folds the feeble hands
of the marionette,
and in her limited life
the whole world is gathered
to its neglected God:
she gathers the whole world

like a contemplative
who, alone in his cell,
gathers the whole world
under the wide wings
of the crucifix—
yet she remains,
with her unique majesty
and her shadowless peace,
in the complete solitude
of adoration.

VII.

We have a law
that one man shall die for the people:
Christ has made Himself subject;
Christ is obedient,
subject even to death—
even the death of the cross.

One shall stand before God
and answer for all:
shall know with the mind of Christ,
shall see with His eyes,
shall utter His words;
shall hear the laughter and tears

of the world with His ears,
shall heal with His hands,
and shall be bound in His burial bands:
one shall love
with the loneliness
of the heart of Christ.

There are a few people confessing their sins—
a whispering like the rustle of rain in leaves.

Each one who brings his story
of tedious little failures,
over and over again,
brings, in his patient hands
and his contrite will,
all who have failed,
all who will not come
to the source to drink.

When the rain falls on one soul
it falls on the parched dust
of the whole world.

When one man is driven
by sorrow for sin
to the Everlasting Arms,

through the dark waters,
his soul is drawn
by invisible light
like a fragment
of broken glass,
worn smooth and round by the sea:
it shines with the strange beauty
of the salt of his sorrow,
and in his single heart
the whole world
is at rest
on the limitless shores of peace,
like a sea-jewel laid at last
by the unresting waves
on the quiet sands in the sun.

A few are confessing their sins:
there is a feathery rustle,
like birds in the wide branches
of an old, spreading tree.

It is the tree whose leaves
open among the stars;
yet its roots thrust down
into the common soil:
it is the tree

where the wild birds nest;
yet its boughs
are the eaves of the house
to the home-loving swallow:
it is the tree whose blossom
is the unfading flower
of the eternal summer;
yet its seed is falling
into the stony ground.

VIII.

In the cathedral,
through ages and ages of men,
the people come and go:
they sorrow, but One endures;
they falter, but One is strong;
they pass, but One remains;
they change, but One is unchanging.

Christ is there
in a corner behind a lamp:
He is in the world
as a man's heart in his breast—
almost forgotten
until a lover

lays her head on the piteous ribs
of the cage of bone
and hears
the mysterious beat
of the pulse of life.

IX.

We have rejected
the yoke that is sweet
and bowed to the yoke of fear:

we have feared discomfort and loss,
pain of body and mind,
the pang of hunger and thirst;
we have been abject
before the opinions of men;

we have been afraid
of the searching ray
of truth;
of the simple laws
of our own life;

we have feared
the primitive beauty

of human things—
of love
and of birth
and of death.

We have lost
the integrity
of the human heart:

we have gone to the dying embers for warmth,
to the flickering lamp for light;
we have set our feet on the quicksand
instead of the rock;

we are the mediocre;
we are the half-givers;
we are the half-lovers;
we are the savourless salt.

Lord Jesus Christ,
restore us now
to the primal splendour
of first love,
to the austere light
of the breaking day.

Let us hunger and thirst;
let us burn in the flame;
break the hard crust
of complacency;
quicken in us
the sharp grace of desire.

Let us not sit content
by the dying embers:
let the embers fall into cold ash;
let the flickering lamp gutter and die;
cover with darkness
the long shadows
thronging the lamp;
make the soul's night
absolute and complete,
the shrine of one star.

Shine in us,
Emmanuel,
Shadowless Light:
flame in us,
Emmanuel,
Fire of Love:
burn in us,
Emmanuel,

Morning Star:
Emmanuel!
God-with-us!

between two worlds
(MAINZ CATHEDRAL, 1936)

Between two wars,
in the Cathedral at Mainz,
an old peasant woman
stands at the foot of the crucifix.

Others pass by,
kissing the wooden feet
of the wooden Christ
as they pass.

Outside in the street
the armies of occupation,
the English soldiers in exile,
march.

The feet of Christ
are nailed.

(Such is the holy will
of Love.)

The hands of Christ,
that give
and bless
and heal,
are nailed back.
(Such is the holy will.)

All day the people pass.
Those of the generation
that somehow escaped war
can bear to look at the blank face
and to kiss the stiff feet
and to push little bunches of flowers
into the dead hands.

The old woman stands
with nothing at all to give,
stands before Christ on the cross,
with her empty heart
and her empty womb
and her empty, open hands
hanging down by her sides.

The German mother
of the defeated soldier,
the son who is dead,
stands still, without tears,
where she has stood
for two thousand years,
in front of the Crucified:

There is nothing at all to do,
mother,
except to forgive.
There is nothing else to do;
everything else is done.

Christ, behold your mother!
Mother, behold your Son!

soeur marie emilie

Soeur Marie Emilie
is little and very old:
her eyes are onyx
and her cheeks vermilion,
her apron wide and kind
and cobalt blue.

She comforts
generations and generations
of children
who are "new"
at the convent school.
When they are eight
they are already up to her shoulder:
they grow up and go into the world;
she remains
forever,

always incredibly old
but, incredibly, never older.

Generations of children
sit in turn by her side
and help her to shell the peas;
her dry and twisted fingers crackle,
snapping the green pods.
Generations of children
sit in turn by her side,
helping to stone the plums
that will be made into jam,
for the greater glory of God.

She has affinity with the hens:
when a hen dies
she sits down on a bench and cries.
She is the only grown-up whose tears,
are not frightening tears;
children can weep,
without shame,
at her side.
She is simple as flax.

She collects the eggs.
They are warm and smooth

and softly coloured—
ivory, ochre
and brown and rose;
they fit the palm of her hand.
Her eyes kindle upon them;
the children, watching gravely,
understand
her dumb, untroubled love.

We have grown up
and gone away
"into the world"
and grown cold
in the service of God.
But we would love Him
even less than we do
if we had never known
Soeur Emilie
with the green peas and the plums
and the hens and the beautiful eggs
and her apron as wide and kind
as skies on a summer day,
and as clean and blue.

in an occupied country

Mother of God,
save the walls of my cottage.
They are only bricks and mortar,
but they embrace
the memory of my son.

War is so cruel!
It not only treads
our children's faces
into the mud
and waters the harvests of sorrow
with their innocent blood,
but it shatters
the four walls
where an old mother
(who asks no more in the end)
could cover her grief.

My home
is only a ruin,
but the four walls are sacred;
they hold and embrace
the memory of my son;
they are the shell
that once was around
my little chicken.

Mother of God,
my Christ's empty tomb
leave me—the walls
of my ruined home.

the blitz train

The people are crowded together,
swaying, rocking, leaning and laughing—
they are seeking a night's sleep.

The train rocks,
and its rhythm says,
over and over again:
"Hush, hush,
do not weep;
all aboard the sleep-train,
all aboard for sleep."

They are seeking one night
touched by the benediction
of white sheets and silence;
but they will come back again

to the twisted iron and stone,
to the gutted hole
that is home,
to the pain
and skill
of the practice
of love.

The windows are blacked out:
they do not see
the defenseless suburbs,
the little egg-shell houses
on either side of the track.

The people are crowded so close
they see each other
only in fragments:
for instance,
a woman's hands on her lap—
her face is hidden—
the hands are asleep;
the fingers uncurl,
wider and wider;
and fall back slowly;
yet remain curled a little,

like the pause
in a flower's dying,
before the petals' falling.

Those hands have relinquished the world:
they have fallen away
from the scrubbing-brush and the broom,
from the pots and pans—
even
from the lapels of the man's coat
in the hour of farewell
in the public station;
they have relinquished their hold
upon life and the lover's life;
they are the meek hands
of Jesus Christ
after the withdrawal of the nails
that nailed them to the cross.

Others cling to that which is dear;
where your treasure is,
there is your heart:
a little boy is clasping a wooden horse;
an old man with long white hair
has a tiny child's high-chair
from a lost Victorian room—

and it may be
that a ghost-child
of frozen snow
sits smiling upon his knee.

A girl has a newborn child,
and a soldier (a stranger to her)
spreads huge hands above
the pip of its face;
his hands are informed with love
for the wonder of life
and its littleness.

A mother of six lugs along
a meal for the family,
and pillows and rugs for them all:
if she must take her brood
through the shadow of death,
and over the River Styx,
so let it be—
but not without a
thermos of hot sweet tea.

Darkness has come outside:
we do not see it,
but know

through the inner voice
that war has made audible;
its shadow,
like shallow waves,
is washing the tired faces.

"Hush, hush,
do not weep;
all aboard the sleep-train,
all aboard for sleep."

From far away,
gathering slowly
and growing,
sweeping the fields
and circling the silence,
the siren sounds.

The train has stopped at a siding,
and someone has opened a door.
Lo! the fields!
delicate grass and clover
in lakes of the light of the moon,
as if the fields were in flood
with shallow and shining water.

Everyone turns to the fields.

How beautiful
are plain and exhausted faces
when they are still and at peace—
as it were, graven in silver:
when trivial thought
and little desire
have been washed away by fire:
how beautiful is the world
to their awakened eyes,
to their awakened minds!

How beautiful they are—
those who are saved by fire—
aware, at last,
of life's loveliness,
among the shadows
in the valley of death!

They are the body of Christ
taken down from the cross:
the nails are withdrawn
from the hands and feet;
they are detached,
even from sorrow;

the crown of thorns
is removed.

They are the body of Christ,
drained out
and for a time
laid by:
but there is Resurrection
everywhere.

The train moves on
and its rhythm says,
over and over again:
"Hush, hush,
do not weep;
all aboard the sleep-train,
all aboard for sleep."

frans

Frans is a refugee,
a Belgian boy.
His eyes are blue forget-me-nots,
opaque, without light.
He has hair like canary feathers.
His face is white.

He walked round
and round and round
a green patch
in a grey London square.
(They had not yet
taken the railings away;
they were still there—
rows of black spears,
hedging the green grass
from the sweet

benediction
of children's feet.)

He spoke his own tongue,
a little *patois*
that no one could understand:
"How shall we sing
the Lord's song
in a strange land?"
He is a creature
of lack-lustre gold
and filigree bird-bones:
his shoulder-blades
show through his coat
like embryo wings.
(Have you ever seen
the antler buds
pushing the furred amber
between the young fawn's ears?)

Where Frans was born,
every year two crops of corn
were wrested from the sandy
soil that thirsted for the sea.

The farmers there
suffered no tree to grow:
they forbade
even the tiny shade
of a green leaf's little hand,
spread between
the sun and the seed,
to bless the land;

the only tree
was the crucifix that stood
by the roadside,
carved in dark wood:
only the crossbeams
made a little shade.

Frans fled down the long white road,
between the fields
without shadow of leaf,
without trees,
saving only the cross.

He fled with a multitude
thronged by the angels,
the holy innocents
and many who fell by the way:

but he is heir
to the promised land;
we have filled a cup
with tears
for him to drink.

Have you ever seen
the field in storm?
the swept torrent of grain
tossed one way,
the swirl and sway
of the flood of gold
in the lash and whip of the rain?

And then
the washed, blue light
and the delicate things that remain
unbroken, after the fury is spent—
the frail, wild flower
with the green thread of a stem,
the web of gossamer hung
between blades of grass,
the chosen ears of wheat?

Frans is the gathered blade;
for him

there is no shadow;
he is chosen for bread:
for the thrashing flail,
for the grinding stone,
for the blanching fire,
for the lifting up
of the Host,
for the draining dry
of the Cup.

He is the peasant-Christ,
carved again
in new
unseasoned
wood,
after the storm of blood.

a prayer to creatures

I beseech you,
be gentle!
Be gentle to the men and to the women
and to the children,
who hold their life in their hands
like a flower.

They have all gathered
the flower of life;
and because it is gathered
it is fading:
it fades swiftly,
like the loveliness of a candle
that is lit.

Dying and flowering
are one thing;

but men, not knowing it,
weep for death.
Be gentle to them.

Each is intent
upon the flower of his own life;
for each it is the secret
of his particular love—
the joy of it and the sorrow:
flesh and blood is consumed in it,
like the wax of the candle
consumed in the flame.

Some lift the blossom up,
like the torch in the runner's hand,
and shower its petals down,
like stars in the darkness.

Some are folded upon it,
devout: like the child on the bus,
home from the one day in the country,
her white face closed in sleep
and a smile of ecstasy
burning quietly through the closed,
sad eyes;
her soul

and her thin body
fending the faint blue light of harebells
brought from the green woods
to fade in the city.

Men and women
and children
pass in endless procession
and are forgotten.
We are among them.
Come, let us pray
that the seed of our life's flowering
fall not upon rock,
fall not upon thorns
or the hard frost
or among weeds;
but that today's sorrow
prepare the world's soil
and sift for sowing tomorrow.

I beseech you,
be gentle!
Because when the flame is lit,
the wax is consumed quickly;
when the leaf flowers,
swift is the withering;

but if the seed fall
into the heart in fallow,
the passing loveliness—
the flicker of light—
will remain in the dark night,
to flower with eternal life.

the adoration of the cross
(WESTMINSTER, 1942)

The world is gathered here,
in the cathedral in Westminster—
men and women and children,
kissing the cross.

How old it is,
the wood of the cross!
How dark it is,
how heavy and sweet!
How wide the wound
in the broken heart!
How fast the nails
in the hands and feet!

This year
the men and women and children
gathered here

are used
to the hard wood:
their lips are bruised already
upon the rood.

They have come from many lands
like birds migrating,
seeking the sun.

They have come from rifled nests,
driven on by a withering wind of death.

Now
they are kissing the cross.

There are dark, brooding faces
glimmering like lit gold;
others, the Northern races,
with blue eyes that are cold,
like frozen water,
but set in ivory-warm,
immobile faces.
The Maltese are there,
with damson eyes
and straight black hair,
and lime-wood features,

pale and smooth and spare;
and soldiers, with their great loads
(one is black,
and tears are in his gentle amber eyes;
he hardly seems to move—
a giant carved in ebony—
even his folded hands
are eloquent with love);

and dark and eager flocks
of children;
refugees,
who whisper, scramble, push
their way to peace:
suffer them
to come to their crumb of comfort,
hand in hand
with that invisible band
of innocents
slain in Jerusalem.

The world is gathered here
in the cathedral
in Westminster.
They have come from many lands,

like birds migrating
through the cold ways of the wind,
one impulse driving them on and on.

Over the scorched earth
and the raped fields,
despoiled of golden grain,
on and on to the sun;
over palls of snow
lying over
the multitudinous face of death,
on and on to the sun;
on and on,
on the wings that spread
on the winds
in cruciform—
on and on to the sun
and to the wings at rest.

But where is the sun
in the city of Westminster?—
patient city of ruins
shrouded in rain.

Where is a nest
for the flight

forward, winged by love,
sweeping down to rest?

It is here:
the sun
is the red halo
ringing the bowed head
of Christ,
of Christ lying dead.

The nest
is here,
on His still breast.

How old it is,
the wood of the cross!
How dark it is,
how heavy and sweet!
How wide the wound
in the broken heart!
How fast the nails
in the hands and feet!

The people are coming up slowly
to kiss the cross—
hardly moving,

because the crowd is so big:
moving slowly,
like waves of a calm sea
gently surging forward,
caressing the quiet shore
with a single wave
that breaks on the steadfast rock,
whose touch disperses
the sea's sorrow of shipwreck
in spray of delicate foam;
like the hair of Mary Magdalene
shining wet with tears
over the feet of Christ.

The world is gathered here,
kissing the cross,
They are not afraid:
they have made the Way of the Cross;
they have nothing to fear any more.
They have carried the cross:
the refugee with his load on his back;
the soldier ready to die—
presanctified
for the sacrifice, bearing his heavy pack;
the boy with the old folk
heavy and slow on his arm,

setting his pace to their pace—
and fast on his track,
steady,
mechanical,
unfailing
steps of Death;
the young mother,
burdened with that most heavy burden
because it is so light—
the fairy weight of the starveling child at her breast;
and the father,
who sleeps as he walks,
and carries his little son
like a sack.

Christ with them,
Christ in them,
strength of them—
every one:
Christ, with His cross on His back.

They have been stripped of their garments:
the home
and the livelihood,
the work of their hands,
and the lovely little lands

where their lives had root;
and the solitude
where, alone with his soul,
man becomes whole.
They have stood
naked, like Christ,
in the hard light of the stare
of the curious,
without hiding for sorrow,
without cover for love.

They have received the nails:
the old folk are nailed
to the strange bed
in the alien land to die;
the mature, to the work
that promised end and repose,
and begins again;
the young, to the sacrifice
that is measureless;
the whole world to pain:
they have made the Way of the Cross.

How old it is,
the wood of the cross!
How dark it is,

how heavy and sweet!
How wide the wound
in the broken heart!
How fast the nails
in the hands and feet!

The people are coming up slowly
to kiss the cross.
They are free,
having nothing;
at peace in a world at war,
and without fear: bowing down low,
kissing the cross—
familiar now—
the cross that those
who have mourned through the ages,
through the ages have blessed.

In a single wave of love,
breaking upon the shore,
they are singing inaudibly,
"Consummatum est!"

The countrymen smile
and whisper,
"Grow, seed,

in the dark earth;
grow, seed, in me!"
The women,
"Increase,
life of the world,
in the barren womb!"

The very old,
who have made friends with death,
"Break, spring;
break
from the ageless tree!"

The soul of the world
is singing, inaudibly,
"I am your tomb,
O Christ!
Christ,
be at rest in me!"

How old it is,
the wood of the cross!
How dark it is,
how heavy and sweet!
How wide the wound
in the broken heart!

How fast the nails
in the hands and feet!

holy saturday (1944)

I.

This morning
the Holy Catholic Church
is lighting the new fire.

Here in this grey London street
a young priest
stands at the door of the church
celebrating the age-long ceremonies
of ageless love.

He lights the incense
in the silver censer,
and a little blue cloud
of adoration
rises to God.

He goes with his acolytes
(an old man too old for war
and a child who is too young)
in grave procession
to the altar.

They walk upon
the scattered petals
of flowers,
bearing a reed
that blossoms with three flames.
And the young voice,
husky with the sweetness
of exultation,
cries out in the morning:
"Lumen Christi!"
"Light of Christ!"

II.

All round the church
there are ruins—
ruins of the home,
ruins of the heart,
ruins of the dreams of men.
And everywhere

there are those
who propose to build
a new world
on the foundation
of ruins.

Everywhere,
those who plan
the Kingdom of God
to the scale
and the mind
of man.

Only the young priest
has no plan.
He is a sower,
sowing seeds of fire
in the furrow
ploughed for the sowing
by sorrow.

He lights a flame
in the heart of man,
in the name
and the power of God.

III.

Lent is over.
Now the world's Lover
wakes in the world again.

Lent is a sleeping spring
in the earth:
the seeding and quickening,
from the sown red
seed of the Lord of Love,
to the season of trees in bud
and the white flower on the thorn.

This Lent
it was harder to see
the folded rose
of the heart of God
in the dry wood.

It is not easy to see
the purple cloak
in the shabbier-day-by-day
drab and grey;
to recognize
Christ
when we do not start

at the sight
of blood and dust
on the human face.

It is not easy to see
the Eternal arms,
wide to the world-embrace,
in the little reach
of man's capacity.
It is not easy to see
Christ crucified
in the crucified human race
when death is commonplace.

Long ago
men carved the crucifix
from the wood of flowering trees—
rosewood, and pearwood, and lime,
and pine, and chestnut,
and walnut and sycamore.
In that time
the skill in the carver's hands
was a sign of the people's
will to adore.

This was the crucifix
in nineteen forty-four:
the artist's eyes fixed and dark,
the poet's tongue black and dumb,
the thinker's mind drained and white,
the pilgrim's feet fixed and still,
the holy hands of the artisan
nailed to a plank,
the imperious will ringed with iron,
the seeing eyes without sight,
the singing tongue without sound,
the creative hands without power,
the loving heart without life—
the Light,
in the dark night
of the world,
dark.

IV.

It is Easter morning.
Christ unwinds the burial bands
and lays them by:
the balm and the spikenard,
the anointing of tears,
the soundless snow

of the white sleep of death,
the body of Christ lays by.

He sets His feet on the dust.
He extends His open hands
with a supreme gesture of love.
He uncovers His heart.

It is not a ghost
who walks in the silver
of morning light;
the shadow that falls on the tombs
is the shadow of a man
of flesh and blood.

It is the shadow
of the virgin's Child,
Who asked her to make Him a heart,
that He might die
to give life.

Now He uncovers His heart.
It has died,
and now He lays it wide
open to life;
He gives it to generations

and generations
of men.

Christ rises from the dead.
There is no salute of guns,
only everywhere in the world
there are men who are aware
of a silence that is audible,
a voice
that is heard only inside the heart,
telling the wordless secret
of ultimate joy.

Everywhere
man is listening
for the first footsteps
of the risen Christ.

He hears
an unseen bird singing
and leaves opening
one by one
in a multitudinous green solitude.

In the silence
he hears the beat

of his own pulse.
It gathers like a tide rising
inside the throbbing in his forehead.
He hears the drumming
of the sap rising
from the roots of the world
and the infinitesimal music
of the tiny hammering
of life under the earth,
and the tap, tap in the egg.

In the red bud of his heart
summer is slumbering,
warm and murmurous
as a swarm of bees,
in heavy honey of golden light.
His heart swells
with a new and secret majesty,
and now he knows
that it is not his own pulse
that he hears in the silence
and feels with his finger-tips
in his thin wrist;
it is the eternal heartbeat
of Absolute Love.

Here is the architect to build the home,
the man whose heart is the home of God.

He is aware of the homelessness
of the Son of Man.
He sees the plan
of the hunted fox's lair,
and of the bird's nest
he apprehends,
with Christ's awakened mind,
the tenderness that made the plan.

HERE is the builder
to build the kingdom,
the man who builds
with the hands of Christ,
the man who loves mankind
with the heart of the risen Christ.

V.

NOW
in the church
the priest is blessing the water.
How beautiful water is!
and selfless.

Christ has made it
miraculous with His life.
It is our birth.

The priest
breathes in the form of a cross
on the beautiful water.
This morning
the Holy Catholic Church
is blessing the fire
and the light
and the streams
of miraculous water
in the four ends of the earth.

It is Easter morning.
Children who are still
as gentle as milk
wake to its wonder;
the children will eat sweets
and sing with angels and birds.
The bells have come home
from Rome
on a flight of silver.

The cock crows.

Once he crowed to make Peter weep,

but now to waken the world.

He stretches his long throat like a ruffled wave of foam.

His scarlet comb,

like a geranium flower,

glows on the blue sky.

Yellow as pollen

the chicken breaks out of his shell.

"Jerusalem,

Jerusalem,

why did you not know,

long ago, the things to your peace?

I would have gathered you

under my wings,

as the hen gathers her chicks!"

The invisible Piper

pipes in the market-place;

the children dance.

The eternal eyes of the Father

kindle with measureless love,

watching the little children

dance to the tune of the Piper.

Over the broken houses
and the wells of the basements,
where a cloud of purple weed
and a young and tender greenness
is growing over the rubble,
long ray of gold
from the rising sun
lengthens and lingers,
like the shadow of God's fingers
in daybreak benediction.

He does not see the world
as a disintegrated race,
parted and separated
by time and place
and generation,
bruised with sin
and ruined with bitter wars.
He does not see each one
as dust, dried up and ready
to fall apart.

Before His holy face
there is one Child only,
the Only-Begotten Son,
in whose risen body

our dark crimson scars
blaze like dancing stars.

This morning
the Holy Catholic Church
is blessing
the new fire.

The cock crows
to wake
the joy of the day.
The yellow chicken
is under the hen's wing.
The children dance before God.
The silver bells ring.
The pure waters of birth
wash the world with light.
The altars are spread
and decked with flowers.
The priest, vested in white,
the Easter Mass begins.

☙

Designed by Fiona Cecile Clarke, the CLUNY MEDIA *logo
depicts a monk at work in the scriptorium,
with a cat sitting at his feet.*

*The monk represents our mission to emulate
the invaluable contributions of the monks
of Cluny in preserving the libraries of the West,
our strivings to know and love the truth.*

*The cat at the monk's feet is Pangur Bán, from the
eponymous Irish poem of the 9th century.
The anonymous poet compares his scholarly
pursuit of truth with the cat's happy hunting of mice.
The depiction of Pangur Bán is an homage to the work
of the monks of Irish monasteries and a sign
of the joy we at Cluny take in our trade.*

"Messe ocus Pangur Bán,
cechtar nathar fria saindan:
bíth a menmasam fri seilgg,
mu memna céin im saincheirdd."

Made in the USA
Middletown, DE
20 April 2023

29028821R00106